SPRING NEXT GENERATION

CORE CONTAINER

J. Scott Stanlick

DEDICATION

I dedicate this book to my goldfish. Actually, I have no fish, but if I did I might like one of those sweet goldfish bowls with one goldfish in it. But who would take it out for walks? This is why I have no pets.

Table of Contents

1 Introduction... 3

1.1 The core container 5

1.2 The rulebook metadata 8

1.3 Creating beans.. 13

1.4 User factories 16

2 Wiring Beans Together 21

2.1 Wiring beans with annotations 26

     2.1.1 The JSR.. 27

2.2 Wiring beans with JSR-330 29

2.3 Qualifying injections 36

2.4 Annotations 37

3 Java Code Configuration.. 45

3.1 Why Java Code for Configuration?.................................. 46

3.2 Combining Java Configurations 50

     3.2.1 Explicit Combining of @Configurations.................. 51

     3.2.2 Implicit Combining of @Configurations 53

     3.2.3 A little twist on @Configurations 54

3.3 Comprehensive boot 56

4 Bean Scope 59

4.1 Singleton scope 60

4.2 Prototype scope 62

4.3 Bean lifecycle.. 65

5 Environment 67

5.1 Environments minus XML.. 71

5.2 Booting an environment.. 76

5.3 @Conditional 78

ACKNOWLEDGMENTS

A huge shout out to all the awesome and beautiful people who work tirelessly to provide the rest of us crazy wicked cool open-source software for free of charge! I make a living on the backs of these giants. I might actually send each and every one of you a fruit basket this year.

Stop staring at me! I'm blank.

1 Introduction

Spring was first introduced in March of 2004. It was designed to handle all the stuff required of an EE scale project so you could focus on your application. It promised a non-intrusive framework that would work using only your simple Java objects and interfaces POJO/POJI.

Most developers I talk to do not even understand the core problem that Spring was designed to solve -- eliminate using the stupid new() operator. If this is you, I would strongly advise that you place a bookmark here and close this book. Now, get yourself the first book in the series titled Thinking in Objects. It is a prerequisite to properly understanding OO and the core Spring container.

If you are reading this, it is presumed you either understand OO pretty well, or have read the first book in this series titled Thinking in Objects. While Spring is comprised of an entire ecosystem of modules and functionality, this book will focus on only those central to the Spring container itself. You can grab the code @ **github.com/stanlick/spring-next-generation** and I keep the latest buzz going @ **springnextgeneration.com**.

Later books in the series will focus on the exotic modules that sit upon this core container.

Core Container is the very center point of the Spring framework. Spring is first and foremost designed to manage your objects using a pattern known as Inversion of Control (IoC). It is analog to the Hollywood principle "don't call us; we'll call you" which means if an object needs other objects, those other objects will be made available automatically via dependency injection (DI). This core functionality happens inside the DI container and is at the heart of all things Spring. This is where the mechanics of creating, preparing and serving up your objects takes place.

This book also covers how to bootstrap the Spring container in an environment specific way. Among the various environments from testing, integration, load testing and all the way to production, Spring can present itself in an environment specific way. We will look at how Spring allows us to easily switch to the environment desired.

Without further ado, let's turn our focus to the Core Container.

1.1 The core container

The first step to knowing Spring is to understand that at its core is the IoC container. This container runs on the Java Virtual Machine and inside it is where all the great Spring things happen. This container is not the same as a server or servlet container. In fact, Spring does not need any type of server at all. I have come to consider the Spring IoC container to be like a chef. Think about a fancy restaurant where you can order meals cooked from scratch and made to order. The chef has plenty of fresh ingredients to choose from and once you order, he blends them together to produce a delicious dish.

I'm getting hungry just thinking about this. We never see the chef but we love what he prepares for us. Now if we substitute plain old java objects for the ingredients and Spring for the chef, we would expect to be able to ask Spring for a fully configured object graph. Let's see what this might look like.

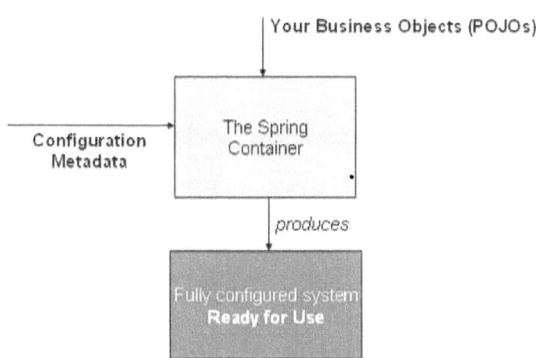

The pieces we are responsible for providing are our POJO's and metadata. Since we have looked at the lambazon.com object model in the last book, we will now discuss the metadata. If you jumped over the first book in the series, don't worry we will again be reviewing the domain model very soon.

If we think back to the chef analogy we can consider the metadata to be his recipes. In object speak, this metadata is the playbook or rules we use to tell Spring how we would like it to manage our objects for us. The way we choose to supply this metadata is flexible and includes XML, Annotations and even writing our rules using Java code. They each have a sweet spot in the technology stack and it really is unwise to expect that one technique will fit every case.

Spring leverages the notion of managing beans in the container. This is not to be confused with EJB; the idea of a bean here is that of the age old Java Bean we now refer to as the POJO. There is absolutely nothing complicated about them at all and kids in 9th grade have fun with them daily. Let's look at lambazon.com and the Customer class.

```
1.  package com.lambazon.domain;
2.
3.
4.  public class Customer {
5.      private Status status = Status.unset;
6.      private OrderHistory orderHistory = null;
7.
8.      private void determinePurchaseStatus() {
9.          status = orderHistory.determineStatus(this);
10.     }
11. }
```

We see that Customer has references to an OrderHistory and Status. Status is an enum so no problem there, but orderHistory currently references null. A call to determinePurchaseStatus() would result in a nasty NullPointerException. We want an instance of

OrderHistory to be wired into Customer, but OrderHistory is merely an interface. We need to determine which implementation should be chosen for instantiation.

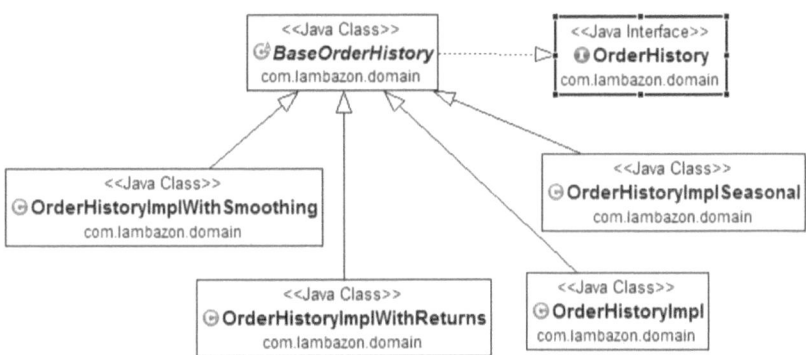

With four implementations to choose from we better talk to a business person about the rules before deciding. Depending on what the business people say about the rules we need to satisfy the injection, we will use one technique or another. Spring has been around awhile and as such has an XML method of feeding it rules that some might consider legacy. Happily there are newer approaches we can use that are more type safe and sane than a wad of XML strings. I will show XML at first so you will at least recognize it if you see it, however, this series will use XML very sparingly and only where it actually continues to make sense today.

The next section discusses how we feed the Spring container our recipe for managing objects.

1.2 The rulebook metadata

The first thing we need to prepare for the chef is the cookbook of recipes and for Spring, the metadata describing how we would like it to prepare, manage and treat our objects. In much the same way that we organize our application into a technology stack along with packaged namespaces, so too will we treat our metadata according to a particular layer of the application. A quick review illustrates the following technology stack for lambazon.com.

We will first use XML to provide our metadata and then move on to annotations and writing our rules using Java code. We start by creating a couple of XML files. One for the overall application called applicationContext.xml and another for our domain objects called domain.xml. The **applicationContext.xml** is the overall application file which contains global metadata and imports the other metadata files. At the moment we have only the domain.xml file in the overall application.

```
1.   <beans
2.       <import resource="domain.xml"/>
3.   </beans>
```

I deliberately omitted the XML namespace and schema stuff as it really doesn't serve much purpose now. The next file is the **domain.xml**.

```
1.   <beans>
2.       <bean id="customer" class="com.lambazon.domain.Customer">
3.           <property name="orderHistory" ref="orderHistory" />
4.       </bean>
5.
6.
7.       <bean    id="orderHistory"
8.               class="com.lambazon.domain.OrderHistoryImplWithReturns" />
9.   </beans>
```

This domain.xml file is where we start to see the "magic". This file has a top level <beans> tag and a couple of bean definitions contained within it. The first things to notice are the two individual bean definitions. The first bean is the Customer and the second is OrderHistory. Notice how each bean has an **id** and a **class** specified. The id is a way to refer to the managed bean from another bean and the class is the type we want to have instantiated. The Customer bean is the more interesting as it is requesting that Spring inject its orderHistory property with a reference to the OrderHistory implementation.

Bootstrapping the Spring container will result in these two objects being created and the order history type being wired into the customer. Let's take a look at the test for this simple configuration.

9

```
1.    @Test
2.    public void bookTwoTestOne() {
3.        ApplicationContext container = new ClassPathXmlApplicationContext("applicationContext.xml");
4.        Customer customer = container.getBean(Customer.class);
5.        assertNotNull("Customer should not be null", customer);
6.        assertNotNull("OrderHistory should not be null", customer.getOrderHistory());
7.        assertTrue("Customer orderHistory should be OrderHistoryImplWithReturns",
8.            customer.getOrderHistory() instanceof OrderHistoryImplWithReturns);
9.    }
```

The first thing we see is the Spring container being created (booted) on line 3. We pass the Spring container our overall application file applicationContext.xml. Once the container starts, we ask it for a managed bean on line 4. On lines 5 and 6 and 7 we have simple regression tests to prove the application is configured properly.

If the business wanted us to instead use the seasonal algorithm to calculate purchases, we would modify **domain.xml** by changing the orderHistory class to OrderHistoryImplSeasonal.

```
1.    <beans>
2.        <bean id="customer" class="com.lambazon.domain.Customer">
3.            <property name="orderHistory" ref="orderHistory" />
4.        </bean>
5.
6.
7.        <bean    id="orderHistory"
8.            class="com.lambazon.domain.OrderHistoryImplSeasonal" />
9.    </beans>
```

And run the following test:

```
1.    @Test
2.    public void bookTwoTestTwo() {
3.        ApplicationContext container = new ClassPathXmlApplicationContext("applicationContext.xml");
4.        Customer customer = container.getBean(Customer.class);
5.        assertNotNull("Customer should not be null", customer);
6.        assertNotNull("OrderHistory should not be null", customer.getOrderHistory());
7.        assertTrue("Customer orderHistory should be OrderHistoryImplSeasonal",
8.            customer.getOrderHistory() instanceof OrderHistoryImplSeasonal);
9.    }
```

We see the different assertion about the injection of OrderHistoryImplSeasonal on line 7. So changing a class name in an XML file changed the runtime complexion of the application. Sweet!

If you are thinking "big deal" then consider this -- real applications contain many more object types than this and having them properly built and wired together is a tricky business. New requirements that modify object models become even more risky. Spring will take care of this brittle aspect of the object system for all of your objects. You essentially feed it your rulebook and let it take care of the object business. When the rules change (and they will) you modify the metadata (not the code) and deploy.

Now that we have a preliminary understanding of how we provide our application rulebook (metadata) to Spring, let's explore a few of those questions you must have burning now. When does the object get created and are they singletons? What if I want to be involved in the object management lifecycle? Yes, those questions and many more. Spring allows you to be involved in the object management lifecycle as much or as little as you wish. For now, rest assured, you have not lost any of your command and control capabilities.

Spring refers to the objects we have it managing for us as BeanDefinition objects. The following table identifies the available metadata available when configuring a spring bean.

id	Unique id
class	Implementation class
name	More later
scope	singleton/prototype/etc
constructor args	Dependency Injection
properties	Dependency Injection
autowire mode	Collaborators
lazy-init mode	More later
init method	Callbacks
destroy method	Callbacks

If you look back at the two beans we configured earlier, you will find we used id, class and properties already. The only real requirement for a managed bean is that it be uniquely identified in the container. If you do not assign a name or id, the container generates a unique name for the bean.

The next section explores the bean configuration and creation in more detail.

1.3 Creating beans

A bean definition is essentially a recipe for creating one or more objects. The container uses your recipe when preparing a managed bean and uses that configuration metadata to create (or acquire) an actual object.

Spring can perform this instantiation itself using either a typical default constructor approach (essentially a reflexive new operator) or through a user factory that you provide. Since Spring is the ultimate factory, you will find it rare that you are feeding Spring your own homegrown factories. If you look back to the Customer and OrderHistory beans we configured earlier, they used the typical default constructor approach. The only expectation is that they contain an accessible empty constructor.

If you require constructor arguments to be injected at object creation time, consider the following. Let's suppose the domain model expects the OrderHistory to be injected via the CustomerWithConstructorInject constructor. The following code illustrates the metadata for this configuration.

```
1.  public class CustomerWithConstructorInject {
2.
3.      private OrderHistory orderHistory;
4.
5.      public CustomerWithConstructorInject(OrderHistory orderHistory) {
6.          this.orderHistory = orderHistory;
7.      }
```

```
1.  <bean      id="customer"
2.            class="com.lambazon.domain.CustomerWithConstructorInject">
3.      <constructor-arg ref="orderHistory" />
4.  </bean>
5.  <bean id="orderHistory" class="com.lambazon.domain.OrderHistoryImplSeasonal" />
```

Notice the CustomerWithConstructorInject has no default constructor. Therefore we are required to specify its constructor arguments in the metadata. In this case Spring would be required to create the OrderHistoryImplSeasonal first. Next, this object will be passed into the CustomerWithConstructorInject constructor.

The following test reveals if we have the correct configuration:

```
1.  @Test
2.  public void bookTwoTestThree() {
3.      ApplicationContext container = new ClassPathXmlApplicationContext("applicationContext.xml");
4.      Customer customer = container.getBean(Customer.class);
5.      assertNotNull("Customer should not be null", customer);
6.      assertNotNull("OrderHistory should not be null", customer.getOrderHistory());
7.      assertTrue("Customer orderHistory should be OrderHistoryImplSeasonal",
8.          customer.getOrderHistory() instanceof OrderHistoryImplSeasonal);
9.  }
```

Unless you have a compelling reason to inject dependencies via constructors, you should really consider using the simple default constructors for your domain types. Just provide your metadata for dependencies and let the container do its job after the empty constructor object is created. In fact, you will discover soon that your POJO domain types do not even need setter methods for the injections. This is the best of all worlds; guaranteed fully-populated objects, no messy constructors and post-construct immutable objects. Bam!

In the spirit of full disclosure, let's discuss the user

factory support. If you have an exotic factory that you want Spring to incorporate into its bean management, the following section is for you.

1.4 User factories

The other approach Spring uses to make objects available is the user factory. There are two flavors of the user factory methods; static and non-static. We will review the non-static user factory and I will leave the static factory for you to review on your own. I do not believe static factories are a good design strategy. Moreover, non-static (instance) user factories can be injected into managed beans and even have injections performed on them!

Let's suppose we have written this magnificent object factory and we were using it before Spring came along. It does these real-time checks to determine the best object at the right time. One such factory method will determine which server in the farm is least busy based on machine loads, solar flares and other critical parameters. We would like Spring to use our user factory for this specific piece of the overall object management.

Our LambazonObjectFactory exposes only a single method as follows:

```
1.  public <T> T get(Class<T> t)
```

This method receives the class of object you would like and returns an implementation of that type. Consider the following client making use of this factory method:

```
1.  Machine bestMachine = factory.get(Machine.class);
```

You will find our LambazonObjectFactory below.

```
1.   package com.lambazon.factory;
2.
3.   import java.util.HashMap;
4.   import java.util.Map;
5.
6.   import com.lambazon.domain.Machine;
7.
8.   public class LambazonObjectFactory {
9.       private Map<String, Object> cache = new HashMap<String, Object>();
10.
11.      public <T> T get(Class<T> t) {
12.          // return best implementation here and cache if appropriate
13.          if (t == Machine.class) {
14.              return getBestMachine();
15.          } else {
16.              return getObject(t);
17.          }
18.      }
19.
20.      @SuppressWarnings("unchecked")
21.      private <T> T getBestMachine() {
22.          // TODO finish me!
23.          return (T) new Machine("127.0.0.1");
24.      }
25.
26.      @SuppressWarnings({ "unchecked", "unused" })
27.      private <T> T getObject(Class<T> t) {
28.          // TODO Auto-generated method stub
29.          return null;
30.      }
31.  }
```

You will find our regression test of this
LambazonObjectFactory below:

```
1.   @Test
2.   public void bookTwoTestFour() {
3.     ClassPathXmlApplicationContext container = new ClassPathXmlApplicationContext
4.               "applicationContext.xml");
5.       LambazonObjectFactory factory = container
6.               .getBean(LambazonObjectFactory.class);
7.       Machine bestMachine = factory.get(Machine.class);
8.       System.out.println(factory);
9.       System.out.println(bestMachine);
10.      assertNotNull("Factory should not be null", factory);
11.      assertNotNull("get(Machine.class) should not be null", bestMachine);
12.  }
```

Now we will consider a Spring managed LoadBalancer
object that can be asked for the "best machine" in the
server farm. This will separate us a level from working
with the factory directly. Realizing that this "best machine"
logic is actually encapsulated in our user factory, we will
need to inject our factory into the LoadBalancer.

```
1.   package com.lambazon.domain;
2.
3.   import com.lambazon.factory.LambazonObjectFactory;
4.
5.   public class LoadBalancer {
6.
7.       private LambazonObjectFactory objectFactory;
8.
9.       public void setObjectFactory(LambazonObjectFactory objectFactory) {
10.          this.objectFactory = objectFactory;
11.      }
12.
13.      public Machine getBestMachine(){
14.          return objectFactory.get(Machine.class);
15.      }
16.
17.  }
```

```
1.    <bean     id="loadBalancer" class="com.lambazon.domain.LoadBalancer">
2.        <property name="objectFactory" ref="factory"></property>
3.    </bean>
4.    <bean id="factory" class="com.lambazon.factory.LambazonObjectFactory" />
```

This is similar to typical objects and dependency injections, however, we see the LambazonObjectFactory being injected into the LoadBalancer is actually serving to create and return the object itself!

```
1.    @Test
2.    public void bookTwoTestFive() {
3.        ClassPathXmlApplicationContext container = new ClassPathXmlApplicationContext(
4.                "applicationContext.xml");
5.        LoadBalancer loadBalancer = container.getBean(LoadBalancer.class);
6.
7.        assertNotNull("LoadBalancer should not be null", loadBalancer);
8.        assertNotNull("Machine associated LoadBalancer should not be null",
9.                loadBalancer.getBestMachine());
10.   }
```

The next example is a more typical usage of the user factory pattern.

```
1.    <bean id="factory" class="com.lambazon.factory.LambazonObjectFactory" />
2.    <bean id="machine" factory-bean="factory" factory-method="getBestMachine"/>
```

Notice that the machine bean metadata does not contain a class and instead specifies a couple of attributes we haven't seen yet. When Spring is asked for a machine, either directly or indirectly, it will defer to the user factory to have the machine chosen. It will call the method getBestMachine() on the factory bean we registered which returns a Machine.

```
1.  @Test
2.  public void bookTwoTestSix() {
3.      ClassPathXmlApplicationContext container = new ClassPathXmlApplicationContext(
4.          "applicationContext.xml");
5.      Machine machine = container.getBean(Machine.class);
6.      assertNotNull("Machine should not be null", machine);
7.  }
```

So we have looked at the two ways Spring can create objects for us -- constructor and user factories. From the point of view of the Spring consumer – your application, it's not apparent who produced the objects. In fact, the recipe from the consumer standpoint is the same. Bootstrap the Spring container with your metadata and ask it for a bean.

The next section is going to concentrate on the more comprehensive job of wiring your managed objects together to produce a well-formed object model.

2 Wiring Beans Together

We saw in the last section how beans were configured and created. We will now look at the more interesting job of wiring these beans together. We know an OO system is a network of collaborating objects, so how is this network of objects created? Let's begin by considering the lambazom.com technology stack and a customer controller.

Domain Model	Request →			Response →	
	Security				
	Cache/Queue/Replicate/Localization				
	Controller				
	Service				
	Repository				
	Persistence				
	Integration				
	Batch				

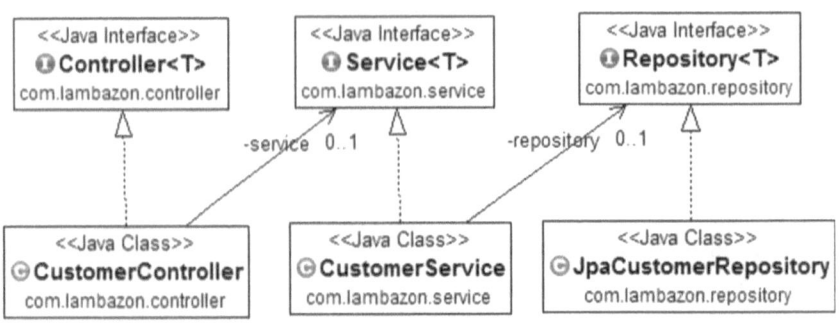

Our interface based design is going to make it a snap to wire the beans together. We see the Controller sends messages to a Service which in turn sends messages to a Repository. But which controller, service and repository implementations will be used? I hope you expect the right ones at the right time. In a real-time world where objects whiz messages around at the speed of the internet, we don't have time to stop and change the software every time a new change comes along; that's how we did it in the 90's man.

Let's begin by considering the XML wiring configuration. We will soon be leaving XML behind and describing alternative techniques, but for now let's simply focus on the mechanics. We are going to keep our roles and responsibilities separate and will create three XML files for our controllers, services and repositories.

We start at the Controller layer. The first pair of illustrations show the Controller<Customer> with a reference to a Service<Customer>. The Spring container will look for a setService(Service<Customer>) method to use for the injection of the service into the controller. *Later we will scrap both the XML and the setter method.*

```
1.    public class CustomerController implements Controller<Customer>{
2.
3.        private Service<Customer> service;
4.
5.        public void setService(Service<Customer> service) {
6.            this.service = service;
7.        }
```

```
1.    <beans>
2.        <bean id="customerController"
3.              class="com.lambazon.controller.CustomerController">
4.          <property name="service" ref="customerService" />
5.        </bean>
6.    </beans>
```

Now we move down to the Service layer. This pair of illustrations show the Service<Customer> with a reference to a Repository<Customer>. Again, Spring container will look for a setRepository(Repository<Customer>) method to use for the injection of the repository which we see in the final repository.xml listing.

```
1.    public class CustomerService implements Service<Customer> {
2.
3.        private Repository<Customer> repository;
4.
5.        public void setRepository(Repository<Customer> repository) {
6.            this.repository = repository;
7.        }
```

```
1.    <beans>
2.        <bean id="customerService"
3.              class="com.lambazon.service.CustomerService">
4.          <property name="repository" ref="customerRepository" />
5.        </bean>
6.    </beans>
```

Finally, we arrive down at the Repository layer. The following repository.xml file shows the bean configuration for our customerRepository. This bean has no dependencies and therefore no nested property tags.

```
1.   <beans>
2.      <bean id="customerRepository"
3.              class="com.lambazon.repository.JpaCustomerRepository"/>
4.   </beans>
```

Now that we have specified our Customer wiring for each of the three layers, we will add these three new XML files to our overall applicationContext.xml file.

```
1.   <beans>
2.
3.
4.      <!-- Global user object factory -->
5.      <bean class="com.lambazon.factory.LambazonObjectFactory"/>
6.
7.      <import resource="domain.xml"/>
8.      <import resource="controller.xml"/>
9.      <import resource="service.xml"/>
10.     <import resource="repository.xml"/>
11.
12.  </beans>
```

We should now be able to test this configuration. The following JUnit test will verify the wiring is correct.

```
1.    @Test
2.    public void bookTwoTestSeven() {
3.        ClassPathXmlApplicationContext container = new ClassPathXmlApplicationContext(
4.            "applicationContext.xml");
5.        Controller<Customer> controller = container.getBean(Controller.class);
6.
7.        Customer customer = new Customer();
8.        assertNull("Customer id should be null", customer.getId());
9.
10.       customer = controller.save(customer);
11.       assertNotNull("Customer id should not be null", customer.getId());
12.
13.       customer = controller.get(customer.getId());
14.       assertNotNull("Customer should not be null", customer);
15.
16.   }
```

Here we bootstrap the Spring container and ask it for a Controller. At the moment we have only a single controller in the container so there is no ambiguity. Once we have a handle to the container managed controller, we are free to send it controller messages. We ask the controller to save a new Customer and then later to retrieve it. Rest assured that before Spring handed us the controller reference, it first created the required service. Following this logic trail, we also appreciate that Spring created the repository our service required. In short, Spring created all the necessary objects and wired them together.

One thing to mention before moving on is the setter methods required for the dependency injections. For those of us who are uncomfortable with mutable objects, stay tuned. In the next section we will turn our attention to an alternate technique that uses annotations as metadata which allows us to get rid of the setter methods. Yay!

2.1 Wiring beans with annotations

We saw in the last section how beans were configured using XML and many shops had to use this approach because it used to be the only choice. Now we have other ways to provide the metadata without XML and its messy, brittle strings. Before discussing this technique, I want to discuss what a JSR is in general and the JSR-330 Dependency Injection more specifically. Surprisingly, many shops I visit are still not familiar with Java Specification Requests.

2.1.1 The JSR

Change is constant and we would like to be able to respond to it swiftly. If you discover your production application is not keeping up with demand, this can often mean a particular technology may need to be replaced with a better choice. Sometimes change comes about because of pricing, new vendors appearing in the space or vendors going out of business. If we are considering this inevitability from the start, we can roll out changes quickly and easily.

The first thing to consider is how tightly you are bound to a particular vendor. If you have imported their packages into your code, you have effectively married them and will need to go through the costly and painful divorce proceedings to separate from them. If instead, you chose to keep the vendor one level removed from your code, then it's a simple "good bye"!

This design technique is nothing new. If you consider what JSR-54 brought to us many years ago, you will see this style of design in action. JSR-54 is the Java Database Connectivity (JDBC) specification that allows us to design to simple interfaces. Connection, Statement, ResultSet, and all the rest are part of JSR-54 and it shielded us from DB2, Oracle, SQL Server, etc. If we designed our application with this JSR in mind then swapping out DB2/400 for Apache Derby didn't require a change to the application. We simply installed Derby and pointed our application to it.

So what is a JSR? It is a vendor neutral specification for solving a technical problem in Java. JSR-330 is the Dependency Injection specification for Java and isolates your domain model from any particular vendor DI container. Spring is not the only vendor in town that wants to manage your objects. Don't get me wrong, I believe Spring is the best one out there and it is my personal choice. However, if Spring-A-Ding-Ding comes along next year and proves to be a better framework, I'd like to plug it into my application and run a load test without going through months of messy divorce proceedings.

The JSR-330 and its partner JSR-250 allow us to annotate aka "rubber stamp" our Java source in a declarative and vendor independent way instead of using all the XML. Consider the following snippet of Customer:

```
1.  import javax.inject.Inject;
2.
3.  public class Customer extends BaseEntity {
4.
5.      @Inject
6.      private OrderHistory orderHistory;
```

Notice the import javax.inject for @Inject. This is vendor agnostic and allows you to plug in whatever DI container works best. Spring is JSR-330 compliant and will dependency inject an OrderHistory managed object into the Customer property orderHistory when it encounters your @Inject annotation. In addition, if we wanted to test drive another DI container, we could swap Spring for say, Google Guice in a matter of minutes. We are talking about plug-n-play at the framework level now. This is a huge benefit to the technology providers – you and me!

2.2 Wiring beans with JSR-330

Spring has proprietary annotations that we could use to provide our wiring recipes, however, we are going to use the JSR-330 annotations instead. We will also examine JSR-250 as we discuss callback methods and participation in the container object lifecycle.

JSR-330 includes six annotations and we typically use only half of them ourselves.

Annotation	Description
@Inject	Inject point
@Named	Managed Bean
@Provider	Provides objects
@Qualifier	Think DSL
@Scope	Bean scope
@Singleton	Injected only once

To demonstrate the annotation method of supplying our metadata recipe to Spring, we will use the same object graph used with XML. This will give us a side-by-side comparison so you can begin to determine for yourself the approach that would work best.

Let's begin by reviewing the lambazom.com technology stack and customer controller.

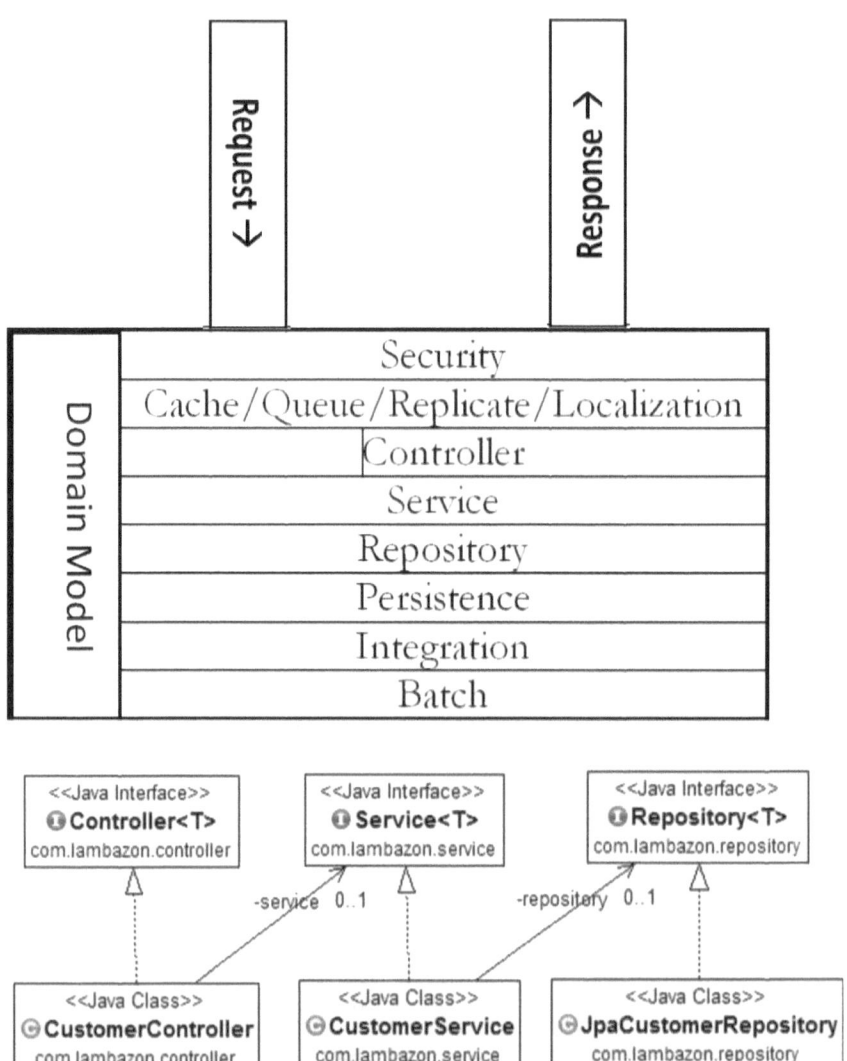

We have now eliminated the XML files, so the only thing to review are the modified Controller, Service and Repository Java files. Each of these objects have been annotated or "rubber stamped" as @Named. This annotation designates them as managed beans so they will be slurped up at boot time and managed by the container. Their id is derived from the class name, with the first character demoted to lower-case. The next thing we see is the @Inject annotation on any dependency that needs to be satisfied. I mentioned the mutability and setter methods required when using XML. When using annotations we can delete the setter methods from the Java files. Object purists love this.

```
1.  @Named
2.  public class CustomerController implements Controller<Customer>{
3.
4.      @Inject
5.      private Service<Customer> service;
```

```
1.  @Named
2.  public class CustomerService implements Service<Customer> {
3.
4.      @Inject
5.      private Repository<Customer> repository;
```

```
1.  @Named
2.  public class JpaCustomerRepository implements Repository<Customer> {
```

Now that we have eliminated the XML files, we will be using a new approach to bootstrap Spring. This new Spring class will create our recipe by scanning for JSR-330 annotation in packages we specify. Once it has rounded our objects up, it works the same as before.

```
1.      @Test
2.      public void bookTwoTestEight() {
3.      AnnotationConfigApplicationContext container = new AnnotationConfigApplicationContext();
4.          container.scan("com.lambazon.annotated");
5.          container.refresh();
6.
7.          Controller<Customer> controller = container.getBean(Controller.class);
8.
9.          Customer customer = new Customer();
10.         assertNull("Customer id should be null", customer.getId());
11.
12.         customer = controller.save(customer);
13.         assertNotNull("Customer id should not be null", customer.getId());
14.
15.         customer = controller.get(customer.getId());
16.         assertNotNull("Customer should not be null", customer);
17.     }
```

Line 4 has Spring scanning for classes in packages rooted at com.lambazon.annotations for our annotations (metadata). And line 5 is technically where Spring comes to life. After this, we interoperate with the Spring managed beans in the same way as we did with XML.

Now let's consider what would happen at Line 7 in a real application where we have several controllers registered. If we had multiple controllers, Spring would complain that we were not being specific enough when asking it for a Controller.class. It would be like walking into the battery store and asking for a battery! So far we have had only a single controller so there wasn't much fuss about which one were going to get.

Spring can work through this ambiguity by using your generically modeled types to determine injections. Let's add another controller for orders and see how Spring can determine one controller from another. I will list both the customer and order controllers here for review.

```
1.   @Named
2.   public class CustomerController implements Controller<Customer>{
3.
4.       @Inject
5.       private Service<Customer> service;
6.
7.
8.   @Named
9.   public class OrderController implements Controller<Order>{
10.
11.      @Inject
12.      private Service<Order> service;
```

We can clearly see they are each Controller types, however, by way of the generics, we can see they differ by what is contained in the diamonds <Customer> and <Order>.

Now we will add our LambazonApplication class and see how this all fits together:

```
1.   public class LambazonApplication {
2.
3.       @Inject
4.       private Controller<Order> orderController;
5.       @Inject
6.       private Controller<Customer> customerController;
```

On line 4 we have annotated our orderController as requiring an injection. This dependency is on a Controller<Order> which is to say not just any Controller, but rather the Controller who has been generically prearranged as the one who controls Order. Likewise, on line 6 we have similar metadata for the customerController. So let's run a unit test to validate our configuration.

```
1.   @Test
2.   public void bookTwoTestNine() {
3.   AnnotationConfigApplicationContext container = new AnnotationConfigApplicationContext();
4.      container.scan("com.lambazon.annotated");
5.      container.refresh();
6.
7.      LambazonApplication application =  container.getBean(LambazonApplication.class);
8.
9.      assertNotNull("Application customerController should not be null",
10.                   application.getCustomerController());
11.     assertNotNull("Application orderController should not be null",
12.                   application.getOrderController());
13.  }
```

Lines 9 and 11 assert that the two controllers were in fact injected into the managed LambazonApplication object. For grins and giggles, I'll list the toString output for you non-believers.

LambazonApplication:
    orderController=OrderController
        service=OrderService
        repository=JpaOrderRepository,
    customerController=CustomerController
        service=CustomerService
        repository=JpaCustomerRepository

You should realize that Spring uses this generic selector algorithm to inject the Services and Repositories down the stack in the same way. I am almost giddy with excitement describing this to you!

Great! But let's raise the bar a little higher. What if we had more than one Controller<Order> in the container? Perhaps we want one for weekdays and another for weekends. In this case we are back to having no unique type for injections and Spring will complain again. You see, Spring is not in the business of flipping a coin when there is a tie!

The next topic is that of object qualification so Spring will be able to resolve our recipe. When we say to Spring we would like greens with our meal, it struggles when looking out at spinach, green beans, broccoli and the other possibilities. Greens are not specific enough.

2.3 Qualifying injections

What if we ask Spring for a bean of some type while it is
managing many distinct beans of the same type? Again
that would be like walking into a battery store and asking
for a battery! The people managing that shop would think
you were nuts.

```
1.  @Named
2.  public class LambazonApplication {
3.
4.      @Inject
5.      private Controller<Order> orderController;
6.
7.      @Inject
8.      private Controller<Order> weekendOrderController;
9.
10.     @Inject
11.     private Controller<Customer> customerController;
```

The LambazonApplication is now requiring Spring to
inject two different order controllers with exactly the same
Java type declarations. The variable names orderController
and weekendOrderController could have been named
anything, so there is no guarantee that we would find a
dependency match on variable name.

I now want to introduce annotations more fully so we
can create our own and understand how Spring and many
other frameworks now depend so heavily on them. We will
use annotations to qualify injection points like the one
above.

2.4 Annotations

An annotation can be thought of as a tattoo. We know there are two types of tattoos; temporary and permanent. One washes off and the other stays with you until the grave. To put this in Java terms, let's consider the following @Override annotation.

```
1.  @Override
2.  public String toString() {
3.      return "LambazonApplication [orderController=" + orderController
4.              + ", customerController=" + customerController + "]";
5.  }
```

You have probably seen this before but did you understand why? This annotation directs the compiler to validate that you are in fact overriding a method with the same signature. It's to help you write safer and more rock solid code.

So let's look at the source code for the @Override annotation and discuss the details.

```
1.  @Target(ElementType.METHOD)
2.  @Retention(RetentionPolicy.SOURCE)
3.  public @interface Override {
4.  }
```

The first thing we notice is that it's just weird! We have seen **class**, **interface** and **enum** types before but what the heck is an **@interface** type? I wonder this myself, but with enough time you will recognize that this is an annotation. It means when you annotate a method with @Override this is what is going on behind the scene. Let's explore the details.

The @Override annotation has been annotated with a couple of annotations itself. This is called a composable annotation, which means annotating an annotation. The first annotation specifies that @Override is only valid to be stamped on a method.

```
1.  @Target(ElementType.METHOD)
```

The next annotation specifies that @Override is only a temporary tattoo. This @Override tattoo is retained only at the RetentionPolicy.SOURCE level. What this denotes is that once the class is compiled (post source) the annotation (or tattoo) is washed off of the object/method. This means the annotations are not verifiable at runtime against the real objects.

```
2.  @Retention(RetentionPolicy.SOURCE)
```

So what does this all mean and who is looking at the annotations anyway? If you think about the @Override annotation, it is clearly a compile time interest and only the compiler is looking for it.

Annotations in and of themselves are a sort of markup language. Something else has to detect the annotations and do the special processing. Annotation Processor Tool (APT) is that detector. First, the APT determines what annotations are present on the source code being operated on. Next, the APT looks for *annotation processor factories* that you have written. The APT asks the factories what annotations they process. Then the APT asks a factory to provide an *annotation processor* for each respective annotation present in source files being operated on. Next, the annotation processors are run. If the processors have generated new source files, APT will repeat this process until no new source files are generated.

Suffice it to say these provided annotation processors do the heavy lifting that we once had to do manually. It will be very rare to find yourself writing one of these processors yourself.

If you know anything about reflection on bytecode then you realize many things can be *determined* about an object at runtime by simply having a conversation with the object itself. Suppose we register a Spring managed bean called OrderControllerChooser that returns the appropriate Controller<Order> based upon the day of week. OrderControllerChooser is going to be injected with all order controllers in the container and we can select a Controller from the Chooser. We could have also written a user factory for this purpose, but we already did that. This is an example of narrowing ambiguous injections with annotations.

The first thing we do is create a java package to contain our custom annotations. Say, com.lambazon.domain.dsl. This will hold the annotations that make up our Domain Specific Language (DSL). The two annotations are listed below:

```
1.  @Retention(RetentionPolicy.RUNTIME)
2.  @Qualifier
3.  public @interface Weekday {
4.
5.  }
6.
7.  @Retention(RetentionPolicy.RUNTIME)
8.  @Qualifier
9.  public @interface Weekend {
10.
11. }
```

These annotations were created so we could tattoo our Order Controllers accordingly. You will see that our annotations have themselves been annotated with the @Qualifier annotation. This is what we call composable annotations. Put another way, Weekend and Weekday are Qualifiers. If you look back at JSR-330, you will see that @Qualifer is part of the Dependency Injection Specification. @Qualifier is designed to overcome ambiguities when more than one of the same type exist in the container. The @Qualifier can also be used to choose between multiple types by way of a particular "tattoo" or annotation.

Now we will tattoo our two Controller<Order> types with their designated weekday/weekend annotation.

```
1.    @Named
2.    @Weekday
3.    public class OrderController implements Controller<Order>{
4.
5.    @Named
6.    @Weekend
7.    public class WeekendOrderController implements Controller<Order>{
```

Lines 2 and 6 markup the two Controller<Order> types so that we can determine which is weekend or weekday.

So now let's look at the interesting parts of OrderControllerChooser (the entire listing is coming up)

```
1.    @Named
2.    public class OrderControllerChooser {
3.
4.        @Inject
5.        private Collection<Controller<Order>> orderControllers;
```

Line 1 @Named makes this a managed bean in the container. This means it can be injected with other beans.

Line 5 is annotated with @Inject so the ordersControllers Collection will be injected with every Controller<Order> type found in the container. Looking at the full source listing reveals how the getController() method determines the correct Controller based upon day of week. The interesting method, isAnnotationPresent(), is how this works. Pay special attention to lines 23 and 32. This is how we can reflect on the object to see it has been tattooed with either our Weekday or Weekend custom annotations.

```
1.   @Named
2.   public class OrderControllerChooser {
3.
4.
5.       @Inject
6.       private Collection<Controller<Order>> orderControllers;
7.
8.       public Collection<Controller<Order>> getOrderControllers() {
9.           return orderControllers;
10.      }
11.
12.      public Controller<Order> getController(){
13.          int dow = Calendar.getInstance().get(Calendar.DAY_OF_WEEK);
14.          if (dow == Calendar.SATURDAY || dow == Calendar.SUNDAY) {
15.              return getWeekendController();
16.          } else{
17.              return getWeekdayController();
18.          }
19.      }
20.
21.      private Controller<Order> getWeekendController() {
22.          for (Controller<Order> controller : orderControllers) {
23.              if (controller.getClass().isAnnotationPresent(Weekend.class)) {
24.                  return controller;
25.              }
26.          }
27.          return null;
28.      }
29.
30.      private Controller<Order> getWeekdayController() {
31.          for (Controller<Order> controller : orderControllers) {
32.              if (controller.getClass().isAnnotationPresent(Weekday.class)) {
33.                  return controller;
34.              }
35.          }
36.          return null;
37.      }
38.  }
```

The unit test for this scenario is as follows:

```
1.   @Test
2.   public void bookTwoTestTen() {
3.       AnnotationConfigApplicationContext container = new AnnotationConfigApplicationContext();
4.       container.scan("com.lambazon.annotated");
5.       container.refresh();
6.
7.       OrderControllerChooser orderControllerChooser =
8.                       container.getBean(OrderControllerChooser.class);
9.
10.      assertNotNull("OrderControllerChooser should not be null", orderControllerChooser);
11.      assertNotNull("OrderControllerChooser should have found Controller<Order>s",
12.                      orderControllerChooser.getOrderControllers());
13.      assertNotNull("OrderControllerChooser should have returned Controller<Order>",
14.                      orderControllerChooser.getController());
15.
16.      int dow = Calendar.getInstance().get(Calendar.DAY_OF_WEEK);
17.      if (dow == Calendar.SATURDAY || dow == Calendar.SUNDAY) {
18.          assertTrue("OrderControllerChooser should have returned WeekendControler",
19.                  orderControllerChooser.getController() instanceof WeekendOrderController);
20.      } else{
21.          assertFalse("OrderControllerChooser should have returned WeekendControler",
22.                  orderControllerChooser.getController() instanceof WeekendOrderController);
23.      }
24.  }
```

We could also have solved this scenario by simply annotating our injection points in LambazonApplication as follows:

```
1.   public class LambazonApplication {
2.
3.       @Inject
4.       @Weekday
5.       private Controller<Order> orderController;
6.
7.       @Inject
8.       @Weekend
9.       private Controller<Order> weekendOrderController;
```

Now we have eliminated the ambiguity by specifying our DSL alongside the injection points. Incidentally, according to the way we named our two controllers and the fact the two private variables happen to match those controller bean names, this would actually work without the custom annotations. However, relying on simple name matching is risky business and the annotations are not that brittle.

This fairly well wraps up the first two styles of providing Spring our metadata or recipe -- XML and Annotations. We even created a couple of our own annotations to qualify injections to one of two possible matches.

In the next section we will look at the final possibility -- writing Java code to provide our metadata. Once you have seen how this works, we'll discuss which techniques work best and at what layers.

3 Java Code Configuration

We have now seen how to provide Spring the metadata about our domain model using XML and JSR-330 annotations. We have also looked at creating our own annotations to qualify injection points where ambiguities were lurking.

In this section we turn to the most recent technique for writing our recipes for Spring -- Java Configuration. The easiest way to think about it is switching out XML for Java. The Java code is not actually executed directly. It is compiled and interpreted or possibly sub-classed by Spring.

3.1 Why Java Code for Configuration?

So why would we use Java code as a means to configure our Spring beans? In a word -- safety! With XML you are dealing with a fat wad of Strings which can be easily misspelled or simply typed wrong. XML is also not included in code refactoring so a change **here** usually causes a break over **there**.

With Java you have type safety. If you enter something wrong, you get a red *X.*   Moreover, Java tooling is very mature so refactoring, documentation, and regression testing are solid right out of the box. Contrast this with XML and you begin to see the stark differences. To illustrate this Java Configuration (safer XML) we will compare XML with the same Java Code Configuration required to configure a simple object. When using JavaConfig, our classes are POJO's and need no annotations.

```
1.   public class Customer extends BaseEntity {
2.       private OrderHistory orderHistory;
```

```
1.   public class OrderHistoryImplWithReturns extends BaseOrderHistory {
```

The following is the XML configuration:

```
1.   <beans>
2.       <bean id="customer" class="com.lambazon.domain.Customer">
3.           <property name="orderHistory" ref="orderHistory" />
4.       </bean>
5.
6.
7.       <bean    id="orderHistory"
8.               class="com.lambazon.domain.OrderHistoryImplWithReturns" />
9.   </beans>
```

And here is the same configuration metadata using Java Configuration:

```
1.   @Configuration
2.   public class SpringConfiguration {
3.
4.       @Bean
5.       public Customer customer(){
6.           Customer customer = new Customer();
7.           customer.setOrderHistory(orderHistory());
8.           return customer;
9.       }
10.
11.      @Bean
12.      public OrderHistory orderHistory(){
13.          return new OrderHistoryImplWithReturns();
14.      }
15.  }
```

It starts on line 1 where the @Configuration annotation makes this a Java Configuration class. On line 4 we see a new @Bean annotation. This annotation is analog to the XML <bean .../> tag. The @Bean annotates a Java method which provides the "metadata" for a bean configuration. Notice how the dependency injection happens on line 7.

Dude, this "by hand" object construction with new() and DI with setter methods is the same old stuff we have been doing for a decade! However, this is NOT inside our Java application code, it's merely our Spring configuration metadata written with Java. On line 11 we see another configured Spring bean. If you do not want to expose the OrderHistory bean, this method could be private and you could remove the @Bean annotation. As it is now, both beans are managed by Spring and can be looked up by and injected into other beans.

The unit test for the scenario is shown below:

```
1.   // @Test
2.   public void bookTwoTestEleven() {
3.       AnnotationConfigApplicationContext container =
4.       new AnnotationConfigApplicationContext(SpringConfiguration.class);
5.
6.       Customer customer = container.getBean(Customer.class);
7.
8.       assertNotNull("Customer should not be null", customer);
9.
10.      OrderHistory orderHistory = customer.getOrderHistory();
11.      assertNotNull("Customer OrderHistory should not be null", orderHistory);
12.  }
```

So what types of things can we do inside a Java @Configuration method? Anything Java! This opens up a very dynamic style of creating and wiring together beans. Suppose we need to find the lowest priced carrier for shipping our orders. This type of dependency injection can only be determined based on shopping the rates in real-time. This is easy to configure using Java Configuration.

In the following example we will walk through the steps to dependency inject the lowest priced carrier into our Shipping object.

```
1.   @Configuration
2.   public class ShippingSpringConfiguration {
3.       @Bean
4.       public Shipping lowestPriceShipping() {
5.
6.           Carrier carrier=null;
7.           //flip a coin to demonstrate the logic
8.           if (Math.random()<0.5) {
9.               carrier = new Carrier("UPS");
10.          } else {
11.              carrier = new Carrier("FedEx");
12.          }
13.          return new Shipping(carrier);
14.      }
```

The first thing we are going to do is break our

@Configuration into components for the various roles and responsibilities. We would never put too much of anything in a single place, so too will we divide and conquer our configurations. You will see how we easily draw them together when it comes time to bootstrap Spring.

ShippingSpringConfiguration has a single @Bean definition on Line 4 called lowestPriceShipping. This bean method determines the lowest priced Carrier, dependency injects it into a Shipping object and returns it. At the moment we are flipping a coin and have a 50% chance of getting either UPS or FedEx. You would clearly put a real web service call or other logic here. Let's see a unit test for this class before combining @Configurations.

```
1.    @Test
2.    public void bookTwoTestTwelve() {
3.        AnnotationConfigApplicationContext container = new AnnotationConfigApplicationContext(
4.            ShippingSpringConfiguration.class);
5.        Shipping shipping = container.getBean(Shipping.class);
6.
7.        assertNotNull("Shipping should not be null", shipping);
8.        assertNotNull("Shipping carrier should not be null", shipping.getCarrier());
9.    }
```

On Line 3 we bootstrap Spring by providing it our new ShippingSpringConfiguration class. After Spring boots it is business as usual. We ask for a Shipping object on Line 5 and validate that both the shipping object and its dependent carrier object have been created.

3.2 Combining Java Configurations

Now that we have seen how SpringConfiguration and ShippingSpringConfiguration work, let's organize the application by roles and responsibilities and provide a single point of bootstrap. There are two ways to do it and I'll show them both.

3.2.1 Explicit Combining of @Configurations

Let's begin by treating SpringConfiguration like we did the applicationContext.xml at the beginning of the book. That is, the single point of entry for the entire application.

Note: this is only for sake of reference and IS NOT needed with Java Configuration.

```
1.  <beans>
2.          <import resource="domain.xml" />
3.          <import resource="data.xml" />
4.          <import resource="controller.xml" />
5.          <import resource="service.xml" />
6.          <import resource="repository.xml" />
7.  </beans>
```

We will begin be creating DomainSpringConfiguration that will provide a central @Configuration for our domain types.

```
1.  package com.lambazon.configuration;
2.
3.  @Configuration
4.  public class DomainSpringConfiguration {
5.      @Bean
6.      public Customer customer(){
7.          Customer customer = new Customer();
8.          customer.setOrderHistory(orderHistory());
9.          return customer;
10.     }
11.
12.     @Bean
13.     public OrderHistory orderHistory(){
14.         return new OrderHistoryImplWithReturns();
15.     }
16. }
```

Now we remove all the @Bean definitions from the SpringConfiguration since they are now in the DomainSpringConfiguration where they belong.

At this point we will see how to use SpringConfiguration as a single point to bootstrap the application.

```
1.  @Configuration
2.  @Import(value={DomainSpringConfiguration.class,
3.                 ShippingSpringConfiguration.class})
4.  public class SpringConfiguration {
5.
6.
7.  }
```

Line 1 still designates this as an @Configuration class, so we can bootstrap Spring with it. The interesting thing to point out is line 2 where we see the @Import annotation. This @Import allows us to pass the array of @Configuration classes that make up the application. This SpringConfiguration brings all of the beans together from Domain and Shipping @Configuration classes. This way we can keep our configurations separated and "role based" and still bring them together at bootstrap time. The following test illustrates this technique:

```
1.  @Test
2.  public void bookTwoTestThirteen() {
3.  AnnotationConfigApplicationContext container = new AnnotationConfigApplicationContext(
4.      SpringConfiguration.class);
5.  Shipping shipping = container.getBean(Shipping.class);
6.
7.  assertNotNull("Shipping should not be null", shipping);
8.  assertNotNull("Shipping carrier should not be null", shipping.getCarrier());
9.
10. Customer customer = container.getBean(Customer.class);
11.
12. assertNotNull("Customer should not be null", customer);
13.
14. OrderHistory orderHistory = customer.getOrderHistory();
15. assertNotNull("Customer OrderHistory should not be null", orderHistory);
```

We bootstrap Spring on Line 3 by passing it our single SpringConfiguration. Notice on Lines 5, 10 and 14 that all beans were managed and passed their tests.

3.2.2 Implicit Combining of @Configurations

The second way to bootstrap Spring from multiple @Configuration classes is by using a "wildcard" scan on your package namespace(s). Provided we had the forethought to identify a package(s) for our Spring Java Configuration classes, this can work very nicely.

```
1.  @Test
2.  public void bookTwoTestFourteen() {
3.  AnnotationConfigApplicationContext container =
4.          new AnnotationConfigApplicationContext();
5.  container.scan("com.lambazon.configuration");
6.  container.refresh();
```

Since we placed all of our @Configuration classes in the com.lambazon.configuration package, this technique is probably simpler than remembering to add any newly created classes to the SpringConfiguration @Import.

The next section reveals an added little twist.

3.2.3 A little twist on @Configurations

It is also possible to dependency inject a configuration class into another configuration class. In the following example we introduce a new configuration class for Order types.

```
1.   @Configuration
2.   public class OrderSpringConfiguration {
3.
4.       @Inject
5.       ShippingSpringConfiguration shippingSpringConfiguration;
6.
7.       @Bean
8.       public Order order(){
9.           Order order = new Order();
10.          order.setShipping(shippingSpringConfiguration.lowestPriceShipping());
11.          return order;
12.      }
```

This new @Configuration OrderSpringConfiguration produces Order types. The ShippingSpringConfiguration @Configuration we discussed earlier is being @Injected into this configuration class on Line 5. When the Order @Bean is requested on Line 8, we see the injected ShippingSpringConfiguration used to inject the lowestPriceShipping into the order.

The following unit test validates the configuration:

```
1.   @Test
2.   public void bookTwoTestFifteen() {
3.       AnnotationConfigApplicationContext container =
4.           new AnnotationConfigApplicationContext();
5.       container.scan("com.lambazon.configuration");
6.       container.refresh();
7.
8.       Order order = container.getBean(Order.class);
9.
10.      assertNotNull("Order should not be null", order);
11.      assertNotNull("Order shipping should not be null", order.getShipping());
12.  }
```

The next section discusses how to bootstrap Spring using a combination of the three metadata styles we have discussed, XML, annotations and JavaConfig.

3.3 Comprehensive boot

In this section we will combine our different recipes (metadata types) into a single comprehensive application. Each of the three recipe styles XML, annotations and SpringConfig have their place in an application and this reveals how to put them all together. To make clear where each bean is configured, I will layout the pieces of our application before running the unit test.

We will begin by creating a file called **data.xml**. This file will contain the metadata for a data source bean.

```
1.    <context:property-placeholder location="classpath:config.properties" />
2.
3.    <bean id="dataSource"
4.        class="org.springframework.jdbc.datasource.DriverManagerDataSource">
5.        <property name="driverClassName" value="${jdbc.driverClassName}" />
6.        <property name="url" value="${jdbc.url}" />
7.        <property name="username" value="${jdbc.username}" />
8.        <property name="password" value="${jdbc.password}" />
9.    </bean>
```

This XML configures a driver manager data source bean called dataSource where the properties are injected with values located in a file called config.properties located on the classpath. The ${} notation is Spring Expression Language and used to plug the variables into values.

Now we will create a **ConnectionPool** bean and annotate it as @Named. The Spring scan() during bootstrap will include this ConnectionPool as a bean managed by the container.

```
1.  @Named
2.  public class ConnectionPool {
3.
4.      @Inject
5.      private DataSource dataSource;
6.
7.      public Connection getConnection() {
8.          return dataSource.getConnection();
9.      }
10. }
```

Notice how the **DataSource** property on Line 5 has been annotated with @Inject. This data source bean is the one we defined in **data.xml**.

Lastly we will create the main Java @Configuration class **AllThreeConfigTypes** that bring everything together. It contributes a bean to the container called **BatchRepository**. This batchRepository needs to be constructor injected with a Connection which will be obtained via the @Injected **ConnectionPool**.

```
1.  @Configuration
2.  @ImportResource("classpath:data.xml")
3.  public class AllThreeConfigTypes {
4.
5.      @Inject
6.      ConnectionPool connectionPool;
7.
8.      @Bean
9.      public BatchRepository batchRepository(){
10.         return new BatchRepository(connectionPool.getConnection());
11.     }
12. }
```

Line 1 identifies this as an @Configuration type. Line 2 is how we combine the **data.xml** into the bootstrap. Line 5 is where we see the **ConnectionPool** being @Injected. And Line 8 reveals a new bean of type **BatchRepository**. Notice how on Line 10 we are using the injected connection pool to inject the batch repository with a connection. Now let's look at the unit test to boot the container.

```
1.   @Test
2.   public void bookTwoTestSixteen() {
3.   AnnotationConfigApplicationContext container =
4.                       new AnnotationConfigApplicationContext();
5.   container.scan("com.lambazon.combined.configuration");
6.   container.refresh();
7.   BatchRepository batchRepository = container.getBean(BatchRepository.class);
8.
9.   assertNotNull("BatchRepository should not be null", batchRepository);
10.  assertNotNull("BatchRepository connection should not be null",
11.                batchRepository.getConnection());
12.  }
```

On Line 3 we create the container using the empty constructor. On Line 5 we scan for annotated files rooted in our base package and on Line 6 we refresh the container. Line 7 shows how the container is ready for business. So we can use the best metadata technique for each layer in our application and combine them all together when bootstrapping the Spring container.

4 Bean Scope

We are now going to discuss bean scopes. Spring has clever defaults that work in many scenarios and require no configuration on our part. However, there are places where only we know how things need to work to satisfy the requirements of our application. One of these places is the bean scope.

The scope of a Spring managed bean determines how many of the beans are created in the container and at what points that decision is made. All of the beans we have wired up so far have been of singleton scope because that is the default scope for a bean unless you say differently. Singleton beans result in the smallest memory footprint for the container and very efficient processing. Think about it, only one bean is created in the container and is simply injected into any dependent bean from there forward.

However, this will not work for all of our beans. For instance, we cannot share a single shopping cart object between thousands of users! Spring provides many scopes out of the box and adding your own custom scope is a simple proposition. We will discuss two scopes now and several more when we reach the book covering Spring Web.

The two scopes we will explore in the next sections are singleton and prototype.

4.1 Singleton scope

We have already hinted at singleton, so let's discuss its prototype. A bean configured with the prototype scope is a bean that will be created anew each and every time it is requested. Realize this bean request could be either direct or indirect. Said another way, you might be asking for bean foo that happens to be @Injected with bean bar. This makes for an interesting conversation as it relates to the scope of each bean involved. Speaking of an interesting conversation, these three guys walk into a bar... Man, I almost went off track there.

Let's create three Spring beans called Foo, Bar and Baz. We will use these beans to illustrate scope and lifecycle.

```
1.   public class Foo {
2.       private Bar bar;
3.   }
4.   public class Bar {
5.       private Baz baz;
6.   }
7.   public class Baz {
8.       private int number;
9.   }
```

We see that Foo needs Bar and Bar needs Baz. Baz will contain a number as we will see in a moment. I omitted the setter methods in these beans because they are ugly and take up too much space on the page.

Do you want to provide the Spring metadata using XML, annotations or Java Configuration? Great, we will use Java Configuration! Our first pass at this configuration metadata is listed below:

```
1.  @Configuration
2.  public class FooBarBazConfig {
3.
4.      @Bean
5.      public Foo foo(){
6.          return new Foo();
7.      }
8.
9.      @Bean
10.     public Bar bar(){
11.         return new Bar();
12.     }
13.
14.     @Bean
15.     public Baz baz(){
16.         return new Baz();
17.     }
18. }
```

Can you tell what the scope of theses beans are? If you said singleton then you are correct! In order to prove things as we go along, let's consider the following unit test:

```
1.  @Test
2.  public void bookTwoTestSeventeen() {
3.      AnnotationConfigApplicationContext container =
4.       new AnnotationConfigApplicationContext(FooBarBazConfig.class);
5.      Foo foo1 = container.getBean(Foo.class);
6.      System.out.println(foo1);
7.
8.      Foo foo2 = container.getBean(Foo.class);
9.      System.out.println(foo2);
10.
11.     assertSame("foo1 should equal foo2", foo1,foo2);
12.
13. }
```

com.lambazon.domain.Foo@73fa5e49
com.lambazon.domain.Foo@73fa5e49

Look at Lines 5 and 8. We ask the Spring container for two beans of type Foo.class and get the same instance twice. The assertion on Line 11 proves this and I also dumped the inherited Object toString() so you can see they each have the same hashcode.

Now let's look at the prototype scope.

4.2 Prototype scope

So let's change the metadata for Foo as follows and run a new test.

```
1.  @Bean
2.  @Scope("prototype")
3.  public Foo foo(){
4.      return new Foo();
5.  }
```

```
1.  @Test
2.  public void bookTwoTestEighteen() {
3.      AnnotationConfigApplicationContext container =
4.       new AnnotationConfigApplicationContext(FooBarBazConfig.class);
5.
6.      Foo foo1 = container.getBean(Foo.class);
7.      System.out.println(foo1);
8.
9.      Foo foo2 = container.getBean(Foo.class);
10.     System.out.println(foo2);
11.
12.     assertNotSame("foo1 should not equal foo2", foo1,foo2);
13.
14. }
```

com.lambazon.domain.Foo@277b65b1
com.lambazon.domain.Foo@16515bb7

Now we have configured the Foo bean with @Scope("prototype"). This changes the nature of how Spring manages this bean in a big way! On Line 12 we see the assertion holds that the two beans are **NOT** the same and again I dumped the toString() output out so you could see the hashcodes are distinct.

Alright, so let's wire the Foo up with a Bar as in the following @Configuration modification.

```
1.  @Configuration
2.  public class FooBarBazConfig {
3.
4.      @Bean
5.      @Scope("prototype")
6.      public Foo foo(){
7.          Foo foo = new Foo();
8.          foo.setBar(bar());
9.          return foo;
10.     }
11.
12.     @Bean
13.     public Bar bar(){
14.         return new Bar();
15.     }
16.
17.     @Bean
18.     public Baz baz(){
19.         return new Baz();
20.     }
21. }
```

On Line 8 we are injecting Foo with a Bar by way of calling the bean metadata bar() method. However, we might have a problem with our Bar bean. Can you see it? Bar is a singleton scoped bean, so even though Foo will be created anew for every request, the Bar bean that it is injected with will always be the same one.

Let's consider the following unit test:

```
1.  @Test
2.  public void bookTwoTestNineteen() {
3.      AnnotationConfigApplicationContext container = {creation here}
4.      Foo foo1 = container.getBean(Foo.class);
5.      System.out.println(foo1);
6.
7.      Foo foo2 = container.getBean(Foo.class);
8.      System.out.println(foo2);
9.
10.     assertNotSame("foo1 should not equal foo2", foo1,foo2);
11.     assertSame("foo1's bar should equal foo2's bar",
12.             foo1.getBar(),foo2.getBar());
13. }
```

The two assertions prove that even though the two **foo** objects are unique, they have each been injected with the one and only **bar** object. This may be what we want, but we may need to scope Bar to prototype.

4.3 Bean lifecycle

This section is going to explain the JSR-250 lifecycle annotations @PostConstruct and @PreDestroy. Spring has a very comprehensive lifecycle that it uses to produce our managed beans; most of the time we will simply use the container and never really think about the object lifecycles at all. However, if your design is such that you have an object that can only be marked "ready for prime time" once you get to "bless it" then the JSR-250 annotations are your way of getting involved in the lifecycle.

All things have a clearly defined birth and death point and Spring beans are no exception. For the sake of this illustration, let's suppose we would like to inspect an Order once it has been fully wired up but just prior to it being handed out to the requester. This is the last possible opportunity to inspect and/or alter it before it is passed out of the container.

```
1.  public class Order extends BaseEntity {
2.
3.      // properties
4.      private Customer customer;
5.      private Shipping shipping;
6.
7.      @PostConstruct
8.      public void applyRules() {
9.          System.out.println("Inside Order.applyRules()");
10.         RulesEngine.process(this);
11.     }
12. }
```

On Line 7 we see the @PostConstruct annotation on a user method. The method applyRules() could be called anything you wish. At this point we have the fully formed order and could make any last minute alterations necessary. Let's suppose we have business rules that apply finishing touches once an object has been fully wired. On Line 10 we pass the order object to a rules engine. The following test results in this output.

```
Inside Order.applyRules()
```
Processing com.lambazon.annotated.domain.Order

```
1.  @Test
2.  public void bookTwoTestTwenty() {
3.      AnnotationConfigApplicationContext container= {creation here}
4.      Order order = container.getBean(Order.class);
5.    }
```

@PreDestroy is the other lifecycle annotation and will signal the container to notify your callback method just prior to destroying an object. This is used far less but can be used to clean up any resources a singleton bean may have created.

5 Environment

This section discusses how to configure and bootstrap the Spring container for a particular environment. I have worked on projects where having 6 to 10 environments was not uncommon and promoting an application from one environment to another was always a messy deal. Between passing program or VM arguments to storing "flags" in files I've seen all the hacks.

Profiles allow a clean way to register different beans during bootstrap according to the desired environments. This feature can help with many use cases:

- Connecting to the right data source
- Test versions of a bean
- Loading customer specific beans (this rocks!)

I worked for a paper company years ago who actually maintained multiple copies of their application to support different clients. And I believe I was part of that crazy decision. Starting the application in the correct mode is made easy using the Spring profile. A profile is just a string and can be anything you like:

- core
- development
- integration
- testing
- production

- customer123
- online
- batch

When bootstrapping the container you specify which profile(s) you would like to be included in the runtime. Any beans **not** associated with a profile **will be** parsed and included in the runtime.

The piece that makes this work is the Spring Environment abstraction. This is where we actually set the profile(s) we want to be "active" on this bootstrap of the container. Let's consider the data source our application might use and discover how we could get the right one for the right environment. The following file is **data.xml**.

```
1.   <beans
2.       <context:property-placeholder location="classpath:config.properties" />
3.
4.       <beans profile="development">
5.           <bean id="dataSource"
6.               class="org.springframework.jdbc.datasource.DriverManagerDataSource">
                 <property name="driverClassName" value="${jdbc.driverClassName}" />
7.               <property name="url" value="${jdbc.url}" />
8.               <property name="username" value="${jdbc.username}" />
9.               <property name="password" value="${jdbc.password}" />
10.          </bean>
11.      </beans>
12.
13.      <beans profile="production">
14.          <jee:jndi-lookup id="dataSource" jndi-name="${jdbc.jndi.name}" />
15.      </beans>
16.  </beans>
```

On Line 1 we see the <beans/> tag as per usual. However, on Lines 4 and 13 we see the <beans/> tag embedded a couple more times! This is to reduce the number of XML files that would be needed if you could only have one profile per XML file. On Line 4 we see the beans in that set (only 1 at the moment) belong to the **development** profile. On Line 13 we see the beans in that set (only 1 at the moment) belong to the **production** profile.

Great! In development we want the embedded database and in production one we locate by looking up JNDI. Now let's look at the ConnectionPool that needs a data source injected into it.

```
1.  @Named
2.  public class ConnectionPool {
3.
4.      @Inject
5.      private DataSource dataSource;
6.
7.      public Connection getConnection() {
8.          return dataSource.getConnection();
9.      }
10. }
```

We will not do anything to this class and I am only showing it so you can see it has a dependency on a data source. So the question becomes which data source does the ConnectionPool need? The answer is always the same - - it depends. The profile(s) we activate will be the beans that come to life.

The active profiles can be specified either programmatically or via a myriad of other choices. Chief among these alternate techniques is declarative using the spring.profiles.active property which can be passed through system environment, JVM arguments, or even context parameters in web.xml. In fact, this property can even be fetched from JNDI!

So let's run a unit test where we set the active profiles

programmatically.

```
1.   @Test
2.   public void bookTwoTestTwentyOne() {
3.       AnnotationConfigApplicationContext container = {creation here}
4.       container.getEnvironment().setActiveProfiles("development");
5.       container.scan("com.lambazon.combined.configuration" );
6.       container.refresh();
7.       ConnectionPool connectionPool =
8.                   container.getBean(ConnectionPool.class);
9.       assertTrue("ConnectionPool should contain",
10.      connectionPool.getConnection() instanceof
11.                                  DriverManagerConnectionSource);
12.  }
```

Line 4 has us setting the active profile to "development." This will result in the ConnectionPool being injected with the DriverManagerConnectionSource. This test is being made on Line 9.

The next test case is for the "production" profile.

```
1.   @Test
2.   public void bookTwoTestTwentyTwo() {
3.       AnnotationConfigApplicationContext container = {creation here}
4.       container.getEnvironment().setActiveProfiles("production");
5.       container.scan("com.lambazon.combined.configuration" );
6.       container.refresh();
7.       ConnectionPool connectionPool =
8.                   container.getBean(ConnectionPool.class);
9.       assertTrue("ConnectionPool should contain",
10.      connectionPool.getConnection() instanceof
11.                                  JndiConnectionSource);
12.  }
```

Line 4 has us setting the active profile to "production." This will result in the ConnectionPool being injected with the JndiConnectionSource. This test is being made on Line 9.

Now let's see how to set environments without XML.

5.1 Environments minus XML

In order to eliminate the fragile XML, I am now going to illustrate working with environments using the new Java Configuration style. Before proceeding though, I want to tell you about my experience thus far with XML while writing this book. I have been creating a profile for each JUnit test method in order to keep my examples and tests synchronized. Now that you know about profiles, I'll let you peek behind the curtain so you can understand my pain. First the bean XML metadata:

```
1.   <beans profile="bookTwoTestOne">
2.      <bean id="customer" class="com.lambazon.domain.Customer">
3.         <property name="orderHistory" ref="orderHistory" />
4.      </bean>
5.
6.      <bean id="orderHistory"
7.            class="com.lambazon.doman.OrderHistoryImplWithReturns" />
8.   </beans>
9.
10.  <beans profile="bookTwoTestTwo">
11.     <bean id="customer" class="com.lambazon.domain.Customer">
12.        <property name="orderHistory" ref="orderHistory" />
13.     </bean>
14.     <bean id="orderHistory"
15.           class="com.lambazon.domain.OrderHistoryImplSeasonal" />
16.  </beans>
17.
18.  <beans profile="bookTwoTestThree">
19.     <bean id="customer"
20.           class="com.lambazon.doman.CustomerWithConstructorInject">
21.        <constructor-arg ref="orderHistory" />
22.     </bean>
23.     <bean id="orderHistory"
24.           class="com.lambazon.domain.OrderHistoryImplSeasonal" />
25.  </beans>
26.        Blah, blah, blah
```

Notice how each little "bean set" is wrapped up in a <beans/> tag and stamped with a profile name bookTwoTestOne, bookTwoTestTwo, bookTwoTestThree. My profile name is exactly the same as my JUnit test case name, so my test cases look like this.

```
1.  @Test
2.  public void bookTwoTestOne() {
3.      ClassPathXmlApplicationContext container = …
4.      container.getEnvironment().setActiveProfiles("bookTwoTestOne");
5.      container.refresh();
6.
7.      Customer customer = container.getBean(Customer.class);
8.  }
9.
10. @Test
11. public void bookTwoTestTwo() {
12.     ClassPathXmlApplicationContext container = …
13.     container.getEnvironment().setActiveProfiles("bookTwoTestTwo");
14.     container.refresh();
15.
16.     Customer customer = container.getBean(Customer.class);
17. }
18.
19. @Test
20. public void bookTwoTestThree() {
21.     ClassPathXmlApplicationContext container = …
22.     container.getEnvironment().setActiveProfiles("bookTwoTestThree");
23.     container.refresh();
24.
25.     Blah, blah, blah
```

Notice how each JUnit test method has the same name as the profile in the XML and each test is activating the case specific profile. So why am I showing you this?

BECAUSE IT IS SO PAINFUL THAT I WANT IT TO STOP NOW!

Trying to keep those brittle Strings spelled correctly in the XML tags has nearly caused me to throw my laptop out of my upstairs window several times this week. I would like to never look at XML again unless it truly makes sense to do configuration there.

Now let us move to the type safe, code complete, compile checking Java IDE that will save my new laptop.

In order to make this environments example a little more fun, we are going to develop a Spring Quiz App where the user (you) can try your hand at answering a few Spring questions. You will be able to specify how difficult you would like the questions to be, so don't freak. This is similar to using the Strategy pattern used in game software. As the player gets better, the game replaces its "rules brain" and becomes a little more difficult.

Let's start by creating a class called Quiz. The Quiz will have a difficulty that you can set according to your level of Spring competency. We will use this difficulty as the profile name that determines what questions to ask.

```
1.  public class Difficulty {
2.      public static final String easy="easy";
3.      public static final String moderate="moderate";
4.      public static final String hard="hard";
5.      public static final String youWillFail="youWillFail";
6.  }
```

I would love to have used an enum here, however it would not play well with the annotations we are about to see. Below is our Quiz class:

```
1.  public class Quiz {
2.      @Inject
3.      private String difficulty;
4.      @Inject
5.      private Questions questions;
6.
7.      private void build(){   }
8.      private Grade grade(){return null;}
9.
10. }
```

The Quiz is annotated to have a level of difficulty and the corresponding questions injected into it. The interesting thing to point out is that Quiz has no idea the difficulty or questions that it will soon contain. At the moment we are not interested in actually grading the quiz, since the difficulty will not affect this grading code.

The interesting bits are in the @Configuration class for our application.

```
1.   @Configuration
2.   public class QuizConfiguration {
3.
4.       @Inject
5.       private Environment environment;
6.
7.       @Bean
8.       public Quiz quiz(){
9.           return new Quiz();
10.      }
11.
12.      @Bean
13.      public String difficulty(){
14.          return environment.getActiveProfiles()[0];
15.      }
16.
17.      @Bean   @Profile(Difficulty.easy)
18.      public Questions easyQuestions(){
19.          Questions<Question> questions = new EasyQuestions();
20.          return questions;
21.      }
22.
23.      @Bean   @Profile(Difficulty.moderate)
24.      public Questions moderateQuestions(){
25.          Questions<Question> questions = new ModerateQuestions();
26.          return questions;
27.      }
28.
29.      @Bean   @Profile(Difficulty.hard)
30.      public Questions hardQuestions(){
31.          Questions<Question> questions = new HardQuestions();
32.          return questions;
33.      }
34. }
```

Line 4 finds this @Configuration object being injected with the runtime Environment. The @Bean on Line 12 is making the active profile available, which will be injected into the Quiz object. Flip back a page and look at the Quiz. Line 7 shows the Quiz @Bean itself. Lines 17, 23, and 29 are the @Beans for each respective degree of difficulty, which will be injected into the Quiz based upon the user selection.

So the user selects the degree of difficulty which in turn becomes the active profile (or environment). This in turn determines which Questions object (easy, hard. etc.) is going to come to life in the container and therefore be injected into the quiz. Brilliant!

Extra credit questions.

- Could you have designed a configuration for this Quiz using qualified annotations instead of @Profiles?
- What if we wanted to create a JpaQuiz? Should Quiz have been an interface? Think generics.
- Would a custom DSL be useful?
- What about @Bean scopes?

5.2 Booting an environment

Now that we understand environments and how we can have several configured and eager to come to life, let's discuss ways to bootstrap a target environment. We saw how to do this in a unit test with setActiveProfiles(). This method takes a variable length String… argument so it is possible to pass more than a single name. This allows us to pass, say ("oracle", "dev") or ("hadoop","dev") and run performance tests on the **same application** environment with **different backend data stores**.

Depending on where the container is being bootstrapped, one of the following techniques might be more favorable than another.

Programmatically:

```
1.    ClassPathXmlApplicationContext container = …
2.    container.getEnvironment().setActiveProfiles("easy");
```

Command line argument:

```
1.  -Dspring.profiles.active="easy"
```

As an initialization parameter in a web.xml:

```
1.  <servlet>
2.    <servlet-name>dispatcher</servlet-name>
3.    <servlet-class>
4.      org.springframework.web.servlet.DispatcherServlet
5.    </servlet-class>
6.    <init-param>
7.      <param-name>spring.profiles.active</param-name>
8.      <param-value>easy</param-value>
9.    </init-param>
10. </servlet>
```

You can also use system environment variables, JVM properties, or look the property **spring.profiles.active** up as an entry on JNDI!

If you still need more control over the beans registered at bootstrap, the next section may be for you.

5.3 @Conditional

If you need more fine grained control than @Profile
provides, you can write your own implementation of the
Condition interface which determines if an @Bean(s) will
be registered in the container or not. The @Conditional
annotation takes your implementation classes as an array.

This is the actual Condition implementation that Spring
uses for @Profile:

```
1.  @Conditional(ProfileCondition.class)
2.  public @interface Profile {
```

```
1.  @Override
2.  public boolean matches(ConditionContext context,
3.                         AnnotatedTypeMetadata metadata) {
4.      if (context.getEnvironment() != null) {
5.          // Read the @Profile annotation attributes
6.          MultiValueMap<String, Object> attrs =
7.          metadata.getAllAnnotationAttributes(Profile.class.getName());
8.              if (attrs != null) {
9.                  for (Object value : attrs.get("value")) {
10.                     if (context.getEnvironment().
11.                         acceptsProfiles(((String[]) value))) {
12.                         return true;
13.                     }
14.                 }
15.                 return false;
16.             }
17.     }
18.     return true;
19. }
```

If the bean is annotated with @Profile, then its value
attribute is looped over and each entry is compared to the
active environment(s) in the context. If any environment
found was NOT an active environment, it is vetoed and
not registered in the container.

Conditions are checked immediately before the bean-definition is due to be registered and are free to veto registration based on any criteria that can be determined at that point.

To make this clear, let's consider the case where we would like beans to be registered based upon the current mode of the system. Rather than pass in the environment as a profile when we bootstrap the container we will let the beans compare themselves to the current machine mode. Hey, somebody may forget to pass the current machine mode as a parameter!

Here are the possible modes the machine can be in:

```
1.  public enum MachineMode {
2.      Unknown, Development, Test, LoadBalance, Integration, Production
3.  }
```

And this is our new annotation for bean metadata:

```
1.  @Retention(RetentionPolicy.RUNTIME)
2.  @Target({ElementType.TYPE, ElementType.METHOD})
3.  @Documented
4.  @Conditional(ModeCondition.class)
5.  public @interface OperatingMode {
6.
7.      MachineMode[] value();
8.
9.  }
```

And this bean holds the current mode of the system:

```
1.  public class CurrentSystemMode {
2.      public static MachineMode currentMode=MachineMode.Unknown;
3.  }
```

Now let's take a look at the Condition class that determines if a bean will be registered or not at boot time.

```
1.  public class ModeCondition implements Condition {
2.
3.      protected static final Log logger = …
4.
5.      @Override
6.      public boolean matches(ConditionContext context,
7.              AnnotatedTypeMetadata metadata) {
8.
9.          MultiValueMap<String, Object> attrs =
10.           Metadata.getAllAnnotationAttributes(
11.                   OperatingMode.class.getName());
12.
13.          if (attrs != null) {
14.              for (Object value : attrs.get("value")) {
15.                  MachineMode[] mode = (MachineMode[]) value;
16.                  for (MachineMode m : mode) {
17.                      if (m==CurrentSystemMode.currentMode) {
18.                          logger.debug(m.name()+" registered.");
19.                          return true;
20.                      } else {
21.                          logger.debug(m.name()+" NOT registered);
22.                          return false;
23.                      }
24.                  }
25.              }
26.          }
27.          return false;
28.      }
29. }
```

Line 9 strips the @OperatingMode annotations off the bean's metadata and the logic to determine if we should register the bean or not is based on whether the metadata is consistent with the current system mode. Now let's look at the @Configuration class and its @Bean metadata.

```
1.  @Configuration
2.  public class ConfigurationForModeCondition {
3.
4.      @Bean @OperatingMode(MachineMode.Unknown)
5.      public MachineMode unknown(){
6.          return MachineMode.Unknown;
7.      }
8.
9.      @Bean @OperatingMode(MachineMode.Development)
10.     public MachineMode dev(){
11.         return MachineMode.Development;
12.     }
13.
14.     @Bean @OperatingMode(MachineMode.Test)
15.     public MachineMode test(){
16.         return MachineMode.Test;
17.     }
18.
19.     @Bean @OperatingMode(MachineMode.Production)
20.     public MachineMode prod(){
21.         return MachineMode.Production;
22.     }
23.
24.
25. }
```

Notice how each bean is annotated with @OperatingMode(). The condition to register the bean or not takes this annotation value and compares it to the current system mode. The following test cases reveal how updating the current system mode results in beans either being vetoed at bootstrap time or registered.

```
1.  @Test()
2.  public void bookTwoTestTwentyFour() {
3.      AnnotationConfigApplicationContext container = …
4.
5.      MachineMode model = container.getBean(MachineMode.class);
6.      assertTrue("Mode should be Unknown ",
7.              model==MachineMode.Unknown);
8.  }
```

The CurrentSystemMode is unknown to start off so this assertion is true. In the next test case pay special attention

81

to Line 3. We must make sure the current system mode is set appropriately BEFORE booting the container.

```
1.  @Test()
2.  public void bookTwoTestTwentyFive() {
3.      CurrentSystemMode.currentMode=MachineMode.Production;
4.
5.      AnnotationConfigApplicationContext container = …
6.
7.      MachineMode model = container.getBean(MachineMode.class);

8.      assertTrue("Mode should be Production ",
9.                  model==MachineMode.Production);
10. }
```

Line 8 reveals the container was running with the production MachineMode this time. I like eggs.

We can also assign our @OperatingMode to an entire group of beans.

```
1.  @Configuration
2.  @OperatingMode(MachineMode.Development)
3.  public class ConfigurationForModeConditionDevelopment {
4.
5.      @Bean
6.      public String foo() {
7.          return "development foo";
8.      }
9.      @Bean
10.     public String bar() {
11.         return "development bar";
12.     }
13.     @Bean
14.     public String baz() {
15.         return "development baz";
16.     }
17. }
```

Line 2 constrains all beans to the Development mode. As you can see, you have much flexibility in booting the Spring container in a way that is tailored to your environment.

The next book in the series will explore Aspect Oriented Programming (AOP). If you are manually coding the same old things over and over, this is a must read.

ABOUT THE AUTHOR

As an author, speaker, musician and software architect, Scott Stanlick is a colorful dude. Scott has been instrumental inside IT shops ranging in size from a few million to many billions of dollars in revenue. He instructs universities and corporations around the world in the application of new technologies and also consults with industry. He enjoys motorcycling and considers people skills his greatest strength.